MUTUAL FUNDS

with

BEN WICKS

BEN WICKS ASSOCIATES

Published in 1994 by
Ben Wicks and Associates
449A Jarvis Street,
Toronto, Ontario,
M4Y 2H2

Note: An investment in any Mutual Fund does not constitute a deposit insured by the Canada Deposit Insurance Corporation or any government deposit insurer and is subject to fluctuations in market value. Past performance may not be indicative of future results. Important information about any Mutual Fund is contained in its simplified prospectus. Please read carefully before investing.

CONTENTS

THANKS, BEN
RR

Acknowledgements

When it was suggested that I write this book my first reaction was one of surprise.
I had completed a book on drug abuse and was about to start on another book related to social problems. A book on matters of finance hardly seemed to fit with the plans I had in mind. However, I was soon convinced otherwise. Money is certainly hard to come by and even harder to hold on to.
Thousands of people who have worked hard to put aside savings are now looking to Mutual Funds in the hopes that their money would at the very least, keep pace with inflation. I was soon convinced that a fun book to help them through the bramble jungle of finance was desperately needed.

Why me, a cartoonist and humorist? In many ways I was the ideal choice. I knew absolutely nothing about finance before starting this book and from this vantage point, was able to pose the stupid questions most of us are frequently hesitant to ask.

But I certainly needed help. Many friends in the world of business were kind enough to answer my questions without laughing out loud. In particular I'm grateful to Ted McConnell, of Barclays McConnell, for suggesting the need for such a book. Tammy Murray, a leading Mutual Funds expert who patiently scanned every suggestion and finally, my editor and researcher, Karen Molson, who spent many hours researching the subject.

Introduction

"Honey, I've been rich and I've been poor," Pearl Bailey once said, "And rich is better."
She was right, it is better.
Knowing that you have money to cushion any future problems that may come your way encourages a distinct feeling of comfort.

Growing up, as I did, in a poor area of London, I have never ceased to be aware that the life I have today is vastly better than the one my parents suffered when I was a child.

Although most of us will never be as wealthy as we would wish, there are many of us who have money put aside "for a rainy day".

Unfortunately in this economic period the sun seems to be forever behind a cloud.

Rainy days are constantly on the horizon ready to force us to loosen our hold on this cash that has been so hard to come by.
There's no denying that this need to hold on is difficult to overcome.

Even worse, as we hold on to what we have, the same hundred dollars that we placed so carefully under the mattress five years ago no longer has the buying power that it once did.

Money that we once put to one side for the day we could finally say "to hell with work, I'm quitting" will today enable us, with luck, to escape for a month before we have to start searching around for another means of earning a living.

So what to do?
We could be like Michael Caine, the movie star. Michael, who grew up in the same area I did, has made a fortune acting and today is a very wealthy man.

As a journalist I remember interviewing him in a tiny trailer during the filming of one of his many movies.

As we discussed mutual friends, it suddenly occurred to me that each of us had been dealt similar cards. Both started out poor, yet he, the movie star, was no longer concerned with money problems.

"What do you do with all your money?", I asked.
"Insurance, dear boy," he answered. "If I fall down the stairs, I'm insured. If I fall out of bed, I'm insured. Whatever happens to me, I'm insured."

What he was saying was that he would never ever again be poor. He had found a way of protecting himself from whatever the future had in store.

Is that what we want and if it is, is that kind of insurance available to us all?
Certainly it is.
But do you really need to be covered for falling out of bed?

Most of us would answer "No!"
Why? For the simple reason that since we do not have the vast sums that enable us to protect ourselves against all eventualities we feel we can hopefully find a better use for the amount we do have.

Let's take a closer look at money and be honest about what it is we think that it can give us.

- Money is the key to bringing the leisure that hides behind a million doors.
- Money makes it possible for us to direct our lives and steer whatever course it is we wish to travel.
- Money enables us to find independence.

So what about that money that we have in our shoe or savings account? Does this money enable us to lead any or all of the above?

Hardly. Since the money that we have held in our shoe for so long is losing its value with each passing day, the answer seems to be that something must be done with it to increase its value or at the very least, keep its value in inflationary times.

The truth is that if we are to find a way of softening any future blows, it's time to get it out from under the mattress or wherever else it is being held for safekeeping and find a way of allowing it to grow. There are various ways we can do this.

We can buy 5,000 lottery tickets. Take a trip to the race track.

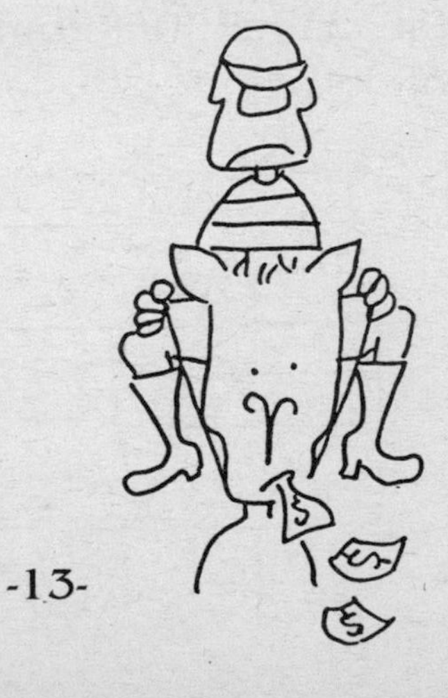

Then again, Las Vegas is just a plane trip away.

Unfortunately each of the above has one thing in common. Each of them asks us to take our money and spend it in such a way as to risk losing what we have.

Hardly a recipe for financial independence. Okay, let's look at another area.

The stock market.
Certainly millions of dollars are made daily by investors who follow the market. Unfortunately millions of dollars are also lost.

Surely this makes the stock market another gamble under a different name. The truth is that it's extremely difficult to predict when a stock that you have bought is about to increase its value.

So why am I even thinking about investing my hard earned bucks in this area?

Because a particular way of investing money in the stock market has seen a dramatic increase in recent years.

The industry that deals in these particular investments has recently topped $105 billion.

What are these investments called and why the interest?
We're about to find out.

AND WHILE IT'S TRUE THAT OUR LORD NEVER HAD TO CONCERN HIMSELF WITH PORTFOLIO DIVERSIFICATION...

1 SO! WHAT ARE THESE THINGS CALLED MUTUAL FUNDS?

Mutual Funds were originally developed to make portfolio diversification available to the average person.

Great. I'm an average person and I haven't the faintest idea what all this means.

Right. It's time to start at the beginning.

Mutual Funds were originally developed to make stock market investing available to all.

With the advent of Mutual Funds it was possible to make a variety of different investing options, ie stocks, bonds or even mortgages, available to the average person.

By investing in a variety of different investments that person would then be achieving "portfolio diversification".

Got it? Okay, it's time to move on and leave behind all the technical jargon.
Let's get directly to the question.

What is a Mutual Fund?
One way to describe it is to break it up and take one word at a time.
"Mutual" means joint or common.
A "Fund" is a pool of money.
So what we have is a pool of money jointly owned.
Whose money?

Some of this money could be yours. Money that you felt you wanted to invest.

So why didn't you invest it?

Because, like many of us, you had no idea where to invest this money.

Stories abound about those who have lost their shirts investing in stocks. And although 1929 was a long time ago, the vision of all those smart people standing on ledges remains with us.

Yet the news persists that in this miserable economy more and more people are entering the market.
Why are they risking their hard-earned bucks in this manner?

For the simple reason that although they know nothing about the stock market, there are those who do. People who are quite prepared, for a small fee, to take your funds and invest for you.

"But surely", you say, "my few thousand dollars, or even hundred dollars, are hardly worth the efforts of an expert".

Wrong! Why?

Because your dollars will join those of others who have felt the same way as you do.

Let's take this particular scenario:

You have decided to take the plunge and feel that it's time to scout around for what is known as a "Mutual Fund family".

There are the Grandparents who are

conservative and have been around
for a good number of years.

They could be the Bond Fund of the family.

Then there is the young twenty-year-old son, who likes fast cars and flash. He could be the Mutual Fund that invests in emerging countries or growth stocks.

And of course, there is Uncle Ben who is a doctor - the solid blue chip Stock Fund.

Different people and different Mutual Funds all make up the "family". Some fast, some slow, and some in-between.

Now all you need to do is a little research to find the Mutual Fund that has a good track record.
Or other people may want to recom-

mend a particular Mutual Fund family, with which they have had good results.
But it should be, one that you are confident can be relied on to meet your needs.

Since more people have decided to hand over their money to Mutual Fund families, investment managers now have thousands of dollars to invest on their clients' behalf.

They have a "pool". A "pool" of money owned by the various people who have decided to place their trust in the experts' hands.

Since it is your money that we are talking about, you will naturally have a few questions to ask.

- How do I go about finding a good Mutual Fund family?

- Can I take my money back if I feel they are not doing a good job?
- Can I take my money back if I find I need it?
- Are there any guarantees?
- How about the risk factor?
- Can I check on how my money is doing at any time I want?

Whoa!
Let's take the questions one at a time. By the time you finish this book you'll have a better understanding of this newfangled thing - a Mutual Fund.

Trust me.
The next time you're at a cocktail party and in need of small talk you could find yourself casually saying, "What do you think about portfolio diversification?"

IF I LOAN YOU A MILLION, I'LL HAVE TO LOAN EVERYONE A MILLION
BANK LOANS

2 I'VE GOT THE BUCKS, NOW, WHAT SHOULD I DO WITH THEM?

Let's start with the good news.
You've got some money.
So what's the bad news?
It's staying at the same
value, or close to it,
as when you first got it.

Maybe Aunt Mary
decided that you
and the local animal
shelter should share

the bundle she left behind.
Or maybe you won a fat prize in a national lottery.

If you're like the rest of us, whichever way you got the money you'd like to hold on to it and hopefully sit back and watch it grow.

It's show time.
Time to watch the performer whose name is on everyone's lips.

Mutual Funds.

At first glance, putting money into Mutual Funds seems like a simple enough thing to do.

"Aunt Mary has left me $10,000. I'll just mosey on down the road and buy me ten thousand dollars worth of them thar Mutual Funds."

Whoa there!
Hold your horses.

Which Mutual Funds are you thinking of buying?

There are hundreds to choose from. You could easily end up throwing a bundle at the very Mutual Funds that are completely wrong for you.

What may appear to be just what you're looking for could turn out to be the disappointment of the century.

Think of it like courting.
It may very well be that the one you're attracted to is not the one who over the years turns out to be Mr. Right.

So how can you tell which of the Mutual Funds is best for you?
By first deciding what your needs are.

In a nutshell, what is it you want your Mutual Funds to do for you?

- Do you want an investment that you can easily convert into cash?
- Do you want your dollars to be invested in the stock market?
  not invested in the stock market?
  or just a little of it invested in the stock market? 
- Do you want your investment to provide you with a regular income?

If your answer to any or all of the above is, "Gee, I...er...maybe if...I don't know ", then your decision to consider investing in Mutual Funds is a good one.

Why?

Because you are about to get guidance - the advice of your own Mutual Fund advisor.

HE WANTS TO
KNOW IF WE
HAVE A MUTUAL
FUND ADVISOR
WITH US

3 WOW! MY VERY OWN MUTUAL FUND ADVISOR!

Before you get too excited about this knight in shining armour who has suddenly galloped over the horizon, you should know one thing. He or she is in business.

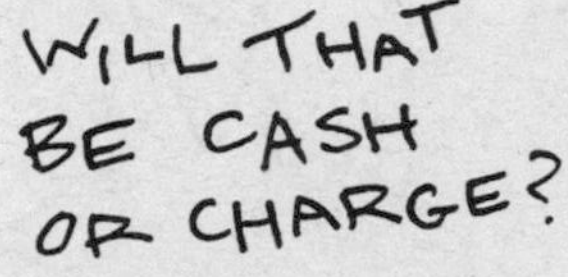

Sure, they're wonderful people but guess what? They also need to eat and they probably have families that are fond of doing the same.

So let's be fair. This is not a boy scout who has taken your arm and helped you across the street.

This is an expert who has spent years studying financial matters so that he or she can help those like us cut our way through the thorny tangle of money management.

Once you have made contact you will find that he or she will be more than happy to help you come to a decision.

As you sit with them, be aware of one thing.
They may wish to probe into what you feel is your personal life.

Don't be disturbed by this. They are just anxious to ensure you invest in the Mutual Fund that best meets your needs.

Then, they will sit patiently and explain- no load, front-end loads, back-end loads, and any other load that you feel may be of interest to you.

It stands to reason that for all their efforts they deserve more than a handshake or a Christmas card for their trouble.

But what is appropriate?
A little something under the saucer when they have finished their tea? Or maybe an extra piece of cake to take home with them as they leave the house?

I hardly think so.

Fortunately there are a set of rules that lay out the customary procedure for us.

There are two ways the Mutual Fund advisor is compensated:-

(1) a sales commission directly from you (known as a "load"); or

(2) by a salary, from his or her employer.

Whether you buy a no-load Mutual Fund, pay a sales commission when you make your first investment, or pay it when you redeem, is up to you.

Once again it depends on which family of Mutual Funds you are buying.

So let's take a closer look at these "loads" and see what they entail.

"Front-End Loads."

Guess what?
This is where you pay up front.

A percentage of the money you put into this type of Mutual Fund is charged as a commission fee.
In other words, a few cents of every dollar you put in comes off the top, or "front-end" of your investment.

"Back-End Loads."

Okay, okay. Yes, the payment

comes off the back end.
But it's a little more complicated than this. The fees are not always calculated in the same way.

Some Mutual Fund advisors will base what they charge on what your initial investment happened to be.

Others will calculate the Fund's market value later.
This can be considerably higher.

"No-Loads."

Simple enough!
You pay nothing to buy these Funds.
Nothing to calculate up front and nothing at the back.

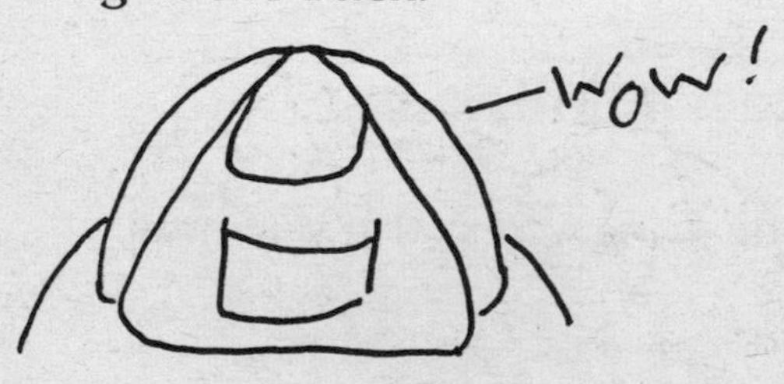

"Management Fees"

There is one fee that all Mutual Funds are charged and that's called a management fee.
This fee is generally taken directly from the "pool" of money in the Fund and is not charged directly to the investor.

It's a Mutual Fund expense and not an investor expense like the "load". This fee covers the costs incurred by the Funds investment manager for making all the investment decisions and operating the Fund.

Just one thing, check carefully, some Funds also charge a host of other expenses directly to the Fund.

FORGET THE TALL, DARK AND HANDSOME STUFF — DO YOU SEE A MUTUAL FUND ADVISOR ANYWHERE?

4 HOW DO I FIND MR RIGHT?

Let's not beat around the bush. We're looking for a Mutual Fund advisor, not someone to take home to meet Mum and Dad.

He can be tall, dark and handsome but if his track record for investing is lousy then it's not only Mum and Dad who will be showing him the door, it's you.

So tall, short, dark, fair, handsome or ugly, the one we're looking for is the one who's going to make our money grow as we paddle our toes in the ocean.

Cutting through all the garbage the one we're looking for is a Warren Buffett.

Who is Warren Buffett? Warren Buffett, my dear friends, is an American who in 1956 went to his family and friends with his hat held out.

The result? $105,100.

Not wishing the effort to appear too one-sided, Warren decided to dig into his own pocket and throw $100 into the kitty.

As manager of a newly formed investment company, Buffett Limited Partnership, Warren decided to pay himself 25% of any profits, making sure that the investors first received a 6-per-cent return on their capital.

How did the investors do?
Over the next 13 years the original investment compounded at 29.5 per cent annually to reach about $100-million.

Finding the right stocks to buy became increasingly difficult for our friend.

By 1969, the market was so difficult to read and stock prices were so high that our honest trader decided to pack up his tent and move on.

Before doing this he gave back most of the money to the shareholders, along with a proportional interest in Berkshire Hathaway, a textile company which he had acquired in 1965.

Okay, so the guy was honest. What did he do for his original investors?

If you had put $10,000 in the original Buffett Limited Partnership then converted it to Berkshire Hathaway your money today would be worth $72-million.

I can hear you now.

You just have one question. When is good old Warren going to be coming around with his hat again?

I'm sorry to disappoint you.

What dear old Warren is worth, no one is sure, but it is roughly $8.3-billion (U.S.)!

So the likelihood of Uncle Warren being in our neck of the woods in the foreseeable future is, I would guess, pretty remote.

So why the hell am I babbling on about Buffett?
We all want a Warren Buffett as our financial advisor. Right?
Okay.
So let's move on.

OKAY, MARTHA, YOU WIN. I'LL QUIT TALKING ABOUT MUTUAL FUNDS— NOW WHERE ARE MY CLOTHES

5 FINDING THE PERFECT MUTUAL FUND FAMILY

Put down the phone. Finding a Mutual Fund family is not going to be difficult. Finding the right one is.

Let's begin by deciding where we're going to look.

Fortunately there are dozens of companies now involved in the business of selling Mutual Funds. Each of them has a staff licensed to sell these popular investments.

Some are investment houses and still others are trust companies and banks that have added this as a service to their customers.

Don't feel that you are alone in becoming interested in this area of the financial world.

In 1993, Mutual Funds exceeded $105 billion. In fact more than 8 million Canadians now invest in Mutual Funds.
So you've certainly got lots of company.

The interest in this form of investment is not surprising in view of the dramatic plunge in interest rates over the past two years.

This has cut deeply into the returns on guaranteed investment certificates and government bonds.

For the traditionally cautious Canadian investor, these had always been extremely popular. Now these same Canadians are looking around for a bigger return on cash that each year seems harder to come by.

Add to this the growing number of Canadians who are working for small companies with no pension plan, and it doesn't take a professor to understand the feeling that more and more people are looking to protect themselves in their later years. Presented with these trends, Mutual

Funds are, in many ways, the ideal financial program for today.

Certainly Mutual Funds allow investors a way of obtaining professional money management to help them understand the growing complexities of today's financial markets. And there's no doubt that we're going to need the help of an expert.

In Canada alone there are more than 700 Mutual Funds so finding our way through this maze is going to need more than a Hansel and Gretel trail of crumbs.

It may help to have some understanding of what it is your Mutual
Fund advisor intends to do with
your money.

There are dozens of options.
He or she may recommend you
divide the money and place some in
cash-type investments, some stocks,
and even some bonds and
mortgages.

"Did you say 'stocks?' But the stock
market is a page in the newspaper
that I pass to get to the Sports
Section."

Fear not. Help is at hand.
Before we decide to go off the high
board, let's just dip our toes in the
shallow end and get a feel for the
kind of pool we're about to enter.

IT'S TIME YOU LEARNED THE FACTS OF LIFE — THIS IS A BILL

6 FINDING YOUR WAY AROUND THE MARKET

When Lorenzo Castelli was struck and killed by a train, the Italian rail-road sued him on charges of delaying rail schedules for twenty-nine minutes.

Like Lorenzo, many of us find that when it comes to finance, whatever happens, seems to have an unhappy ending.

It may ease your mind to know that you are not alone.
When it comes to money matters, many of us feel as though we should stay in bed and pull the covers over our heads.

We don't understand the world of dollars and cents, but we do know that we have money that we would like to keep.

There was a time when the answer to what we should do with our loot was fairly easy to answer.

Just put it in the bank where it's safe and we can watch it grow.

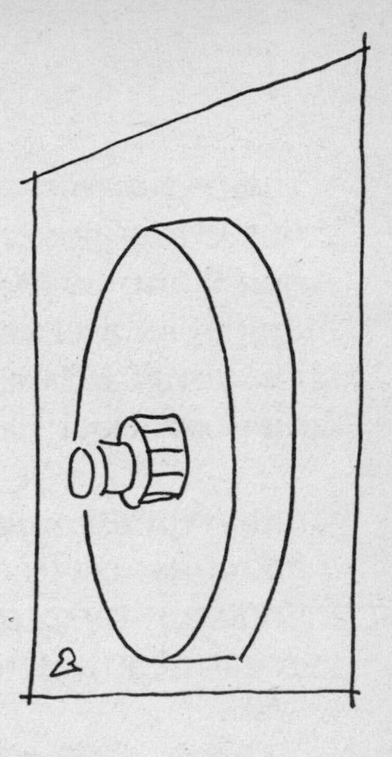

Although this continues to be the choice of many, the fact is that the growth rate today is a lot different than that of the past.

Since the government has decided that everyone is happy to live in a world of low interest rates, many find themselves in a position of being able to borrow money at an extremely low rate of interest.

This is fine for those who wish to borrow; however, if we are fortunate enough to find ourselves with money that we wish to invest, then I'm afraid we find ourselves in a different boat.

Although it's true that the banks are about as risk-free as you can ever hope for, the growth of the deposit is not nearly as great as many would wish.

Fortunately there are other forms of investment that can give a greater return that involve investing money in shares and before you head for the exit, never to return, you'd be wise to listen up and know a little about this mysterious animal known as "The Market".

Any newly formed business, big or small, needs money and whoever the owners are they will be required to invest their own cash.

As proof of their investment they will receive shares equal to their investment. If each investor puts up $500 and there are ten investors, the company issues 5,000 shares, five hundred to each investor.

If you were one of the share owners, you now own a percentage of the company. If the business grows and makes money, then each of the owner's shares grows in value.

If the business begins to lose money, then each of the shares lose value.

Some large companies sell shares to the general public. These shares can then be bought and sold on an international stock exchange, such as the Toronto Stock Exchange. This can involve thousands of investors and millions of shares being issued.

In cases like these, many factors can influence the value of the shares.

Maybe a company has just landed a huge contract and is expecting a growth in profits.

The shares of this company will jump in expectation of that profit.

On the other hand, if a company is experiencing problems and is forced to lay off employees, the value of the shares of this company could begin to fall.

Maybe a large number of share-holders will decide that they wish to sell their shares and switch their money to something else.

This could result in a large number of those shares being available for sale and once again result in a share loss.

It's the law of supply and demand and is no different in the world of the stock market than anywhere else.

If you are one of those who is a stranger to the market and wish to become involved, the territory can be extremely unfriendly.
What you need is someone to steer you through the many pitfalls and along with others, spread out your risks.

Someone who is quite willing to explain the various ways of getting to where you want to go.
And more than this, find that when you arrive, you're

in better shape than when you left.

The main problem for the investor speculating on the stock market is one of available funds.

In order to get involved, an investor generally needs to buy at least 100 shares at a time.
Even if we could afford to buy a large number of shares of one particular company, is this wise?

If that one company does not grow or begins to lose money, your investment has been a bad one.

A closer look at the entire stock market will reveal the obvious. Some companies make money and others lose it.

Yet as a general trend, there is growth.

Since placing all your eggs in one basket is not recommended, spreading your investment around is usually the wise thing to do - portfolio diversification.

Unfortunately many of us do not have sufficient funds to allow us to do this, so we look to a Mutual Funds manager.

Someone who has been trusted with sufficient money from others who will be happy to add our money to theirs and invest it in various areas that will ensure growth.

WHY IS HE
HOLDING AN
INSTANT BANK CASH
CARD IN HIS HAND?

7 Before We Start, Are There Any Questions?

There's just one thing I want to remind you of before you sit down to chat with your new Mutual Fund advisor.

What we're talking about is your money, not someone else's.

Since it's yours, it's important that you're the one who's going to decide what to do with it.

So if you feel like asking questions and are not sure what to ask, here is a little background on the discussion you'll be having.

Although there are many different types of Mutual Funds there are just four basic types:

"Cash-Type Funds".

These are Funds which invest in money market investments, such as Treasury Bills.
Many like them for the simple reason that they are known as the safest type of Mutual Fund available.

Understand that by "safe", I mean the least risky as an investment.

Why are they known as "safe"? Because with "cash-type" Mutual Funds your money will find its way into the buying of assets that have the most consistent track record, or rate of return.

Then why isn't everyone throwing their cash at this type of Fund?

Because in taking a low risk on an investment, such as this, you can expect less interest or return on your money.

That's fair. Those who decide to throw their dart at a target the size of a barn door, should get a smaller prize for hitting it than those who are throwing their dart at a bullseye the size of a penny.

On the other hand, these "cash-type" Mutual Funds are the easiest kind to cash in whenever you feel in need of some ready cash.

So to sum up.
If you're looking for a safe, short-term investment, then "cash-type" Mutual Funds are for you.

"Fixed Income Funds".

These are a type of Mutual Funds that deal with investments that pay a set rate of return.

Your money will quite possibly be used to buy what are considered, "sure things", such as bonds and mortgages.

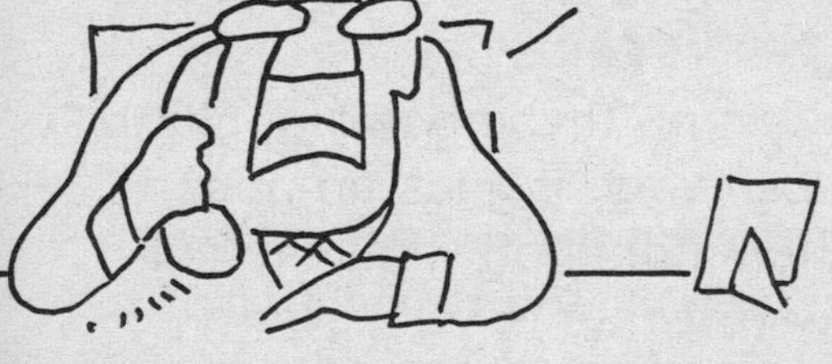

The good news is that, not only can you expect a steady flow of income from these investments, but these types of Mutual Funds are likely to yield a better rate of interest than the "cash-type" Mutual Funds.

But there is a down side...just a little, no cause for alarm.
Your money has been invested in a market commodity that fluctuates.

The return on these types of Mutual Funds can vary: it goes up and down depending on what the current interest rate is.

"Growth Funds".

"Boy!" I can hear you saying. "Just the kind I was looking for! Ones that grow." Don't unzip your wallet yet.

This group of Mutual Funds is mostly tied in with the stock market, although some of them may also be involved with commodities, precious metals and real estate.

It's true that these kinds of Funds are not as safe or conservative as the first two we described, but on the other hand, if you're willing to take the risk, the returns can have you sending out for the bubbly.

"Balanced Funds".

Now we're into the most popular type of Mutual Funds.
If you thought Madonna had fans, then you should see the numbers that line up when Balanced Funds make an appearance.
And it's not difficult to see why.
Like Madonna, it's all in the performance.

Balanced Funds combine the best of all other types of Mutual Funds.
Once invested your money will find itself being spread around like a wisp of cirrus cloud on a clear blue summer's day.

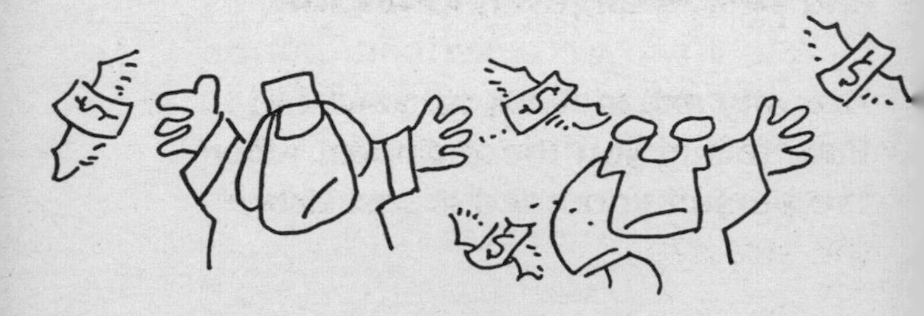

All manner of combinations can come into play.
The money may be divided into some cash-type investments, some stocks, and even some bonds and mortgages - it's a family of Mutual Funds, all tucked into one compact Fund - no fuss, no muss.

Why would we want our money venturing into so many areas? Because, my dear friend, the spreading out of your funds in this way can achieve even higher returns and best of all, even lower risk.

But why am I taking up valuable time telling you these things, when the person you need is just down the street?

AS THE DAYS DWINDLE DOWN TO A PRECIOUS FEW I SAY TO HELL WITH CANADA SAVINGS BONDS

8 WHAT YOU NEED IS A GRANDPA

My Grandfather had a glass eye fitted after his eye was kicked out by a horse. A vase that sat on the mantelpiece contained his money. Once asked why he always placed his glass eye beside the vase, he answered, "It's there to keep an eye on my money!" Like my Grand-father's glass eye, the Mutual Fund advisor is there to keep an eye on your money.

So if you feel like asking questions and are not sure what to ask, here is a little background on the discussion you'll be having.

Q. What's the difference between closed and open-ended Funds?
A. Open-ended Funds have an unlimited number of units for purchase and can grow to any dollar size. The only way you can buy into a closed-ended Mutual Fund once all the units are sold, is to buy from someone who owns units and for whatever reason, wishes to sell.

Q. How do I find such a deal?

A. These Mutual Fund units are listed on the stock exchange where they can be bought and sold.

Q. How will I know the price I'll need to pay?

A. The selling price of a closed-ended Fund is set by the market. This means that its value will be determined by supply and demand and sometimes means that it sells for less than its current "net asset value", or true worth.

You should know that most Canadians avoid the closed-ended type of Funds and select the open-ended version.

Q. So, what are open-ended Mutual Funds?

A. When you buy into open-ended Mutual Funds, you are buying shares or units, along with a number of others also buying units directly from the Mutual Fund company. The number of units offered depends on the number of people wanting to buy them. The price you pay to buy or sell in an open-ended Fund is the current price on that day - no bidding or asking on the stock market - but it's true worth.

With closed-ended Funds, a limited number of units are offered for sale. With open-ended Funds, there is no limit, and the more investors there are in an open-ended Fund, the larger the Fund becomes.

Q. How do I find out how much my units are worth at any one time?

A. You can check directly with the Fund company where you obtained the units, or check the newspaper. The prices are listed daily. Multiply the current price of your Fund by the number of units you own - that's how much your investment is now worth.
Simple!

As the value of the whole Fund grows, so does your particular share. The beauty of all this is that at the same time, your money in the Fund is being reinvested back into the Fund and is compounding.

Q. What if I decide to sell my units?

A. Then the selling price is based upon the current value of the Fund at the time you decide to sell.

Q. If another Fund interests me, can I switch Funds?

A. Mutual Funds usually allow their investors to transfer funds from one Fund to another; however, some Funds may charge you a fee to transfer. Remember the "Back-End Load"?

Q. If my Mutual Fund goes down in value, should I sell it right away?

A. You can expect the value of your Mutual Fund units to fluctuate on a regular basis. The important thing to remember is that most of these will be short term changes, and their investment value is a long-term consideration. In other words, with time, significant growth should be expected.

If, however, for more than a year your units have been generating a return that is lower than you would like, it may be time to review your portfolio and possibly shift your money to another Fund.

Q. Can I make cash withdrawals from my Mutual Fund?
A. A wide variety of withdrawal plans are available within most Mutual Funds. These can range between lump sum withdrawals, to plans that enable you to receive certain amounts of cash on a regular basis over a certain amount of time.

Q. Are there any guarantees or insurance on my investment?
A. No. Mutual Fund shares or units are not insured by the Canada Deposit Insurance Corporation nor guaranteed by the Mutual Fund company.

You'll notice that there has been no mention of taxes.

Q. Does this mean I don't pay any taxes on profits from Mutual Funds?

A. (I must say one thing about you, the reader. You have a good sense of humour.) No such luck - unless you invest in Mutual Funds as part of your RRSP or RRIF.

TWO PINTS—
THAT SHOULD
COVER YOU
FOR ANOTHER
YEAR.

TAX DEPT

9 OH, NO. HERE COMES THE TAX MAN!

The Plainsfield, New Jersey, police reported that a burglar kicked in the rear door of Mrs. Wilma Barnett's home and stole a television set, the kitchen clock, and Mrs Barnett's full-grown German Shepherd watchdog.

Those of us who pay taxes know how Mrs. Barnett must have felt. We have had the same problem with the tax man.

Nothing escapes their attention. Certainly the income from Mutual Funds as well as Canada Savings Bonds, or any non-sheltered investments we make, has long ago felt the glare of their evil eye.

They know that there are three ways in which Mutual Funds can make investment income.

Since the tax rules and calculations will be different for each type of Mutual Fund income, all they need to know is which one it is that you've bought into.

For instance. Was your Mutual Fund formed around a trust agreement or was it incorporated?

Let's start with Mutual Funds set up as trust agreements - they're the most common type.
The trust itself usually does not pay taxes because the income generated goes directly to the investors in the Fund.

You would receive a payment likely once a year that is known as a "distribution", and this payment would include interest income, dividends, capital gains or any combination.
You will then receive a T-3 tax slip detailing how this all breaks down for the tax man.

When a Mutual Fund is set up as a corporation, it must pay taxes as any company would, but the tax rate is much lower than for an individual.

However, the company would avoid paying this tax directly to the government by passing its income directly to its shareholders, who are then responsible for the tax. You will receive a T-5 tax slip.

Some Mutual Funds offer built in tax advantages. You can easily ask your Mutual Fund advisor about these.

And one other thing.
Tax laws change.

Make sure that you ask your Mutual Fund advisor about these changes and how they may affect your investments.

Conclusion

I have tried my best to make this book as much fun to read as I could.
Obviously the secret to any successful book is that the reader should want to turn the page.

In addition to turning each and every page, it is my wish that you now have some knowledge of Mutual Funds.

However, do remember that a little knowledge can be a dangerous thing.

Although you are certainly better informed than you were, I would advise you to seek help before investing your hard earned funds.

Mutual Funds are not a way to get rich quick but if you decide, with the help of an expert, to invest regularly, according to every study that has been done, you will beat inflation.

Whatever you decide to do in your newly found world of Mutual Funds, enjoy yourself.

And if at times your Funds are not doing what you hoped remember Mrs. Vera Czermak of Prague.

After hearing that her husband was leaving her for another woman Mrs. Czermak flung herself from a third-story window. Mrs Czermak was taken to hospital, where she quickly recovered.

Mr. Czermak, upon whom she'd landed, was killed instantly.

So however dark
one day may appear to be, there's always a silver lining somewhere.